# Wedding Planner Playbook

By J. Hilton Dies

A Newbiz Playbook Publication

J. Hilton Dies retains the exclusive rights to any use and training applications of the Wedding Planner Playbook

Wedding Planner Playbook. Copyright© 2016 by newbizplaybook.com All rights reserved. Printed in the United States of America. No part of this book may be used or reproduced in any manner whatsoever without written permission except in the case of brief quotations embodied in critical articles and reviews. For information address Newbiz Playbook Publishers at **products@newbizplaybook.com**

FIRST EDITION

ISBN 978-1539339892

**For downloadable tools emailed directly to you please email products@newbizplaybook.com use the password newbizwedding in the re: of the email**

Copyright – This product is produced in Microsoft Word format to allow for ease of use by the product purchaser. It may not be reproduced, sold, or otherwise distributed in whole or in part to any third party.

For my family, the answer to my why

## Understanding Your "Product"

The fundamental truth about wedding and event planning is that the product is, for those who hire you, a dream. Many of the people looking for your expertise have imagined this moment for a substantial part of their lives. Your task is to deliver that perfect day. One of the biggest mistakes that new wedding and event planners make is to try to use low prices, or the perception of discounted value to attract customers. Your customers don't want the cheap option, and what's more they will be less likely to hire someone offering it.

People who hire professionals for this service are looking for an elite experience, for you that means incredible responsiveness. You provide a cell phone. You answer emails within hours if not minutes. For that your customers will pay a premium. Your image, dress, tone, and interactions create this experience.

Nordstrom's is not an inexpensive store. Their products are expensive, even more expensive than other stores by a fair margin, but their client service and return policies are exceptional. The Ritz Carlton hosts very nice facilities, but honestly for the cost, they are not materially better than many less expensive hotels. The difference is in service, and the way they make their patrons feel.

Ignore this fundamental truth, and none of these contents will matter. Embrace it, and you will succeed. The goal is to create Raving Fans at every opportunity. The clients you help will have friends and family getting married, and you want them to insist on you to handle them.

## How to Charge For Your Services

Hourly – These packages include a set number of hours driven by a budget agreed upon by the client. , planners' rates range from $75 to more than $150 per hour. Consulting packages typically are billed by the hour and consist of the client sitting down with the wedding planner and asking questions based on the area or areas they need help in. This may be pulling together design ideas, confirming or suggesting vendor or venue choices or ensuring that the client is on track and has not forgotten anything. These types of meetings typically take place early in the planning process. These meetings are a great opportunity for the wedding planner to upsell the client and recommend a Day of Coordination or even a Full Service wedding package. Luckily for you, many times the client will realize they really do need more help than they had originally thought. However, these recommendations should be reserved until after the session has completed, as the client is paying you for your expertise, not your sales pitch.

Daily – Some clients want to be more involved in the planning of their event, and hire a wedding or event planner to manage details on the day of the event. Charges for these events range from $1000 to $2000 dollars to manage the event for the day. Although this package is typically booked well in advance of the wedding, the wedding planner does not get involved until 1-2 weeks prior to wedding day.

As a day of coordinator, responsibilities include creating a detailed timeline, contacting the vendors for formal introductions, confirming day of contact information and reviewing copies of all contracts to clarify all contractual obligations of all vendors. After discussing the client's vision for their ceremony, the wedding planner would be in charge of running the wedding rehearsal. And on the day of the wedding their responsibilities would be to be present at the venue and ensure every detail is set up the way the client has envisioned it.

As a Day Of Coordinator, you should also be the liaison between the bride and the vendors for the day. This greatly relieves the bride of unnecessary stress, which is, in a nutshell what being a wedding planner is really all about. During the ceremony and reception, the wedding planner's responsibility is to ensure everything runs smoothly. The goal is to adhere to the timeline, but in the event that this isn't possible it is the wedding planner's responsibility to ensure that events are rearranged in such a way that incurs minimal cost and stress to the bride, groom, their families and their guests.

The package cost for Day of Coordination can vary widely depending on the area of the country, the size of the wedding and if there are one or two locations.

Full-service planners range from $3,000 to more than **$10,000**, depending on experience and demand. In some instances these are flat fee engagements, and in others the fee is a percentage of the total wedding cost ranging from 10-20%. Many wedding planners who are well-established will only do full service since this gives them full control of the look and feel of the wedding that they are putting their names (and reputations) on.

In this package, the wedding planner is practically running the show from conception to execution. Full service wedding planners recommend the vendors, which gives them the opportunity to work with vendors they are familiar with and can trust. They also typically are very involved with the planning of the décor, flowers, linens, rentals and printed materials. They also take care of all of the details included in the Day of Coordination package.

# Percentage Contingent Agreement

CLIENT-PLANNER AGREEMENT

This Client-Planner Agreement entered into this_____day of _____ by and between _____ ("Planner") and _____Client.

Client desires to engage planner to perform event planning services for a_____and said planner desires to perform these event planning services for the event on_____.

SECTION 1. SERVICES: Planner shall organize and co-ordinate all mutually agreed upon service as set forth in Addendum A. The forgoing shall be collectively known as services.

SECTION 2. COMPENSATION AND PAYMENT: The following fees shall apply.

2.1 Client shall pay planner 15% (fifteen) of the total event cost to provide the services referenced in Addendum A.

2.2 The total sum of all fees for each service provided as set forth in Addendum A.

2.3 Any additional charges plus planner's 15% (fifteen) for services requested by the client that is not included in the initial contract fee.

2.4 Reasonable and necessary lodging and travel expenses actually incurred. Upon receipt of an expense report with supporting documentation (invoices). No travel or lodging expense shall apply for events within a 25 (twenty five) mile radius of downtown

City_____State_____ all such expenses in excess of $50 (fifty) and travel plans must be approved in advance by the client.

▪ 2.5 $50% (fifty) of the total contract fee including services and planner's fee upon execution of this agreement. 25% (twenty five) 1 (one) month prior to the scheduled event. 25% (twenty five) 5 (five) days prior to the event.

▪ 2.6 Full contract fee shall be due and owing upon signing of this agreement.

▪ SECTION 3: TERMINATIONS: The effective date here of shall be the date upon which the last party to the agreement signs the agreement. It shall remain in effect until all obligations under the agreement have been completed.

▪ 3.1 Either party to the agreement may terminate his (her) agreement with or without cause providing at least 60 (Sixty) days written notice to the other party. The planner will refund any client monies paid minus (-) cost and planner's fees already incurred.

▪ 3.2 CLIENT CANCELLATION: Within 60 (sixty) days of the event are subject to full planner's fee, charges up to the date of the cancellation in addition to any cost incurred.

▪ 3.3 PLANNER CANCELLATION: Within 60 (sixty) days of the event are subject to full client refund of monies paid Minus (-) non-refundable deposits or charges.

▪ SECTION 4: CONTRACTS SIGNING: Planner shall not enter into any contracts on behalf of the client. The planner will provide the client with information including costs, contracts, and service provisions for potential service providers. The client will establish all necessary contracts within the time frame as set forth by the desired service provider.

▪ SECTION 5: INDEMNIFY (Secure against hurt). Except as otherwise prohibited by law each party shall indemnify and hold the other party harmless from all claims, actions, suits, losses, and expenses of any nature for its employees or subcontractors, breach of their agreement, negligence or intentional misconduct.

⁂ SECTION 6: GOVERNING LAWS AND VENUE: This agreement shall be governed by the laws of the state of _____ (Your Company's home state). Client and planner consent and agree that any legal action or proceedings arising hereunder shall be brought there.

⁂ SECTION 7: NOTICES: All notices, modifications, demands, requests or other communications given pursuant to this agreement shall be given in writing and shall be deemed to have been given if delivered by hand, facsimile or certified mail, effective upon receipt of such notice, demand, request or other communication and signature by both parties.

The Client and Planner each cause this Agreement to be executed in their respective names. All as of the last date written below:

SMITH'S EVENT

CLIENT
SIGNATURE_____

PLANNER
SIGNATURE_____

NAME_____

NAME _____

# Hourly Rate Agreement

CLIENT-PLANNER AGREEMENT

This Client-Planner Agreement entered into this_____day of _____ by and between _____ ("Planner") and_____Client.

Client desires to engage planner to perform event planning services for a_____and said planner desires to perform these event planning services for the event on_____.

SECTION 1. SERVICES: Planner shall organize and co-ordinate all mutually agreed upon service as set forth in Addendum A. The forgoing shall be collectively known as services.

SECTION 2. COMPENSATION AND PAYMENT: The following fees shall apply.

☐ 2.1 Client shall pay planner an hourly rate of _____ to provide the services referenced in Addendum A.

☐ 2.2 The total sum of all fees for each service provided as set forth in Addendum A.

☐ 2.3 Any additional charges plus planner's 15% (fifteen) for services requested by the client that is not included in the initial contract fee.

☐ 2.4 Reasonable and necessary lodging and travel expenses actually incurred. Upon receipt of an expense report with supporting documentation (invoices). No travel or lodging expense shall apply for events within a 25 (twenty five) mile radius of downtown

City_____State_____ all such expenses in excess of $50 (fifty) and travel plans must be approved in advance by the client.

⬜ 2.5 $50% (fifty) of the total contract fee including services and planner's fee upon execution of this agreement. 25% (twenty five) 1 (one) month prior to the scheduled event. 25% (twenty five) 5 (five) days prior to the event.

⬜ 2.6 Full contract fee shall be due and owing upon signing of this agreement.

⬜ SECTION 3: TERMINATIONS: The effective date here of shall be the date upon which the last party to the agreement signs the agreement. It shall remain in effect until all obligations under the agreement have been completed.

⬜ 3.1 Either party to the agreement may terminate his (her) agreement with or without cause providing at least 60 (Sixty) days written notice to the other party. The planner will refund any client monies paid minus (-) cost and planner's fees already incurred.

⬜ 3.2 CLIENT CANCELLATION: Within 60 (sixty) days of the event are subject to full planner's fee, charges up to the date of the cancellation in addition to any cost incurred.

⬜ 3.3 PLANNER CANCELLATION: Within 60 (sixty) days of the event are subject to full client refund of monies paid Minus (-) non-refundable deposits or charges.

⬜ SECTION 4: CONTRACTS SIGNING: Planner shall not enter into any contracts on behalf of the client. The planner will provide the client with information including costs, contracts, and service provisions for potential service providers. The client will establish all necessary contracts within the time frame as set forth by the desired service provider.

⬜ SECTION 5: INDEMNIFY (Secure against hurt). Except as otherwise prohibited by law each party shall indemnify and hold the other party harmless from all claims, actions, suits, losses, and expenses of any nature for its employees or subcontractors, breach of their agreement, negligence or intentional misconduct.

▢ SECTION 6: GOVERNING LAWS AND VENUE: This agreement shall be governed by the laws of the state of _____ (Your Company's home state). Client and planner consent and agree that any legal action or proceedings arising hereunder shall be brought there.

▢ SECTION 7: NOTICES: All notices, modifications, demands, requests or other communications given pursuant to this agreement shall be given in writing and shall be deemed to have been given if delivered by hand, facsimile or certified mail, effective upon receipt of such notice, demand, request or other communication and signature by both parties.

The Client and Planner each cause this Agreement to be executed in their respective names. All as of the last date written below:

SMITH'S EVENT

CLIENT                              PLANNER
SIGNATURE_____             SIGNATURE_____

NAME_____                   NAME _____

# Flat Fee Agreement

CLIENT-PLANNER AGREEMENT

This Client-Planner Agreement entered into this_____day of _____ by and between _____ ("Planner") and_____Client.

Client desires to engage planner to perform event planning services for a_____and said planner desires to perform these event planning services for the event on_____.

SECTION 1. SERVICES: Planner shall organize and co-ordinate all mutually agreed upon service as set forth in Addendum A. The forgoing shall be collectively known as services.

SECTION 2. COMPENSATION AND PAYMENT: The following fees shall apply .

2.1 Client shall pay planner a flat fee in the amount of _____ to provide the services referenced in Addendum A.

2.2 The total sum of all fees for each service provided as set forth in Addendum A.

2.3 Any additional charges plus planner's 15% (fifteen) for services requested by the client that is not included in the initial contract fee.

2.4 Reasonable and necessary lodging and travel expenses actually incurred. Upon receipt of an expense report with supporting documentation (invoices). No travel or lodging expense shall apply for events within a 25 (twenty five) mile radius of downtown

City_____State_____ all such expenses in excess of $50 (fifty) and travel plans must be approved in advance by the client.

▫ 2.5 $50% (fifty) of the total contract fee including services and planner's fee upon execution of this agreement. 25% (twenty five) 1 (one) month prior to the scheduled event. 25% (twenty five) 5 (five) days prior to the event.

▫ 2.6 Full contract fee shall be due and owing upon signing of this agreement.

▫ SECTION 3: TERMINATIONS: The effective date hereof shall be the date upon which the last party to the agreement signs the agreement. It shall remain in effect until all obligations under the agreement have been completed.

▫ 3.1 Either party to the agreement may terminate his (her) agreement with or without cause providing at least 60 (Sixty) days written notice to the other party. The planner will refund any client monies paid minus (-) cost and planner's fees already incurred.

▫ 3.2 CLIENT CANCELLATION: Within 60 (sixty) days of the event are subject to full planner's fee, charges up to the date of the cancellation in addition to any cost incurred.

▫ 3.3 PLANNER CANCELLATION: Within 60 (sixty) days of the event are subject to full client refund of monies paid Minus (-) non-refundable deposits or charges.

▫ SECTION 4: CONTRACTS SIGNING: Planner shall not enter into any contracts on behalf of the client. The planner will provide the client with information including costs, contracts, and service provisions for potential service providers. The client will establish all necessary contracts within the time frame as set forth by the desired service provider.

▫ SECTION 5: INDEMNIFY (Secure against hurt). Except as otherwise prohibited by law each party shall indemnify and hold the other party harmless from all claims, actions, suits, losses, and expenses of any nature for its employees or subcontractors, breach of their agreement, negligence or intentional misconduct.

▢ SECTION 6: GOVERNING LAWS AND VENUE: This agreement shall be governed by the laws of the state of _____ (Your Company's home state). Client and planner consent and agree that any legal action or proceedings arising hereunder shall be brought there.

▢ SECTION 7: NOTICES: All notices, modifications, demands, requests or other communications given pursuant to this agreement shall be given in writing and shall be deemed to have been given if delivered by hand, facsimile or certified mail, effective upon receipt of such notice, demand, request or other communication and signature by both parties.

The Client and Planner each cause this Agreement to be executed in their respective names. All as of the last date written below:

SMITH'S EVENT

CLIENT
SIGNATURE_____

PLANNER
SIGNATURE_____

NAME_____

NAME _____

## Planning Checklist

This checklist is intended to be used both in the actual planning of the wedding and in the pre-engagement discussions that give rise to the scope of work to be agreed between the parties. It should be included as an attachment for Addendum A to the agreement to describe items to be handled by the planner.

## Checklist

The following checklist is an ideal timetable. Couples who do not have as much time as shown should plan their wedding in much the same order, using the checklist as a guide. Be sure to check things off as they are completed.

### Immediately after the engagement:

- _____ Hire photographer.
- _____ Get engagement photo taken.
- _____ Prepare engagement analysis.
- _____ Discuss a budget and the size and style of the wedding and determine who/which family will pay for various aspects of the wedding. Key decisions about number of guests, and scope should be discussed.
- _____ Consider making lists of who must be invited, who should be invited, and who it would be nice to invite to help narrow the guest list.
- _____ First pass at wedding party including ring and flower bearers
- _____ Evaluate venues, and check availability if inside 18 months.
- _____ Make arrangements for the music at the wedding and reception.
- _____ Make all transportation arrangements to and from the wedding.
- _____ Make arrangements for passports if needed

- \_\_\_\_ Choose a wedding date and time.
- \_\_\_\_ Create a binder to organize your thoughts, photos, worksheets, etc.
- \_\_\_\_ Make initial contact with vendors and obtain references.
- \_\_\_\_ Meet with clergy member; schedule pre-marital counseling.
- \_\_\_\_ Reserve wedding and reception sites; make initial catering contacts.
- \_\_\_\_ Consider color palettes and dress for parties at wedding.
- \_\_\_\_ Register at local bridal registries.

## Six months or more before:

- \_\_\_\_ Finalize the guest list.
- \_\_\_\_ Send out Save the Date cards.
- \_\_\_\_ Reserve a block of hotel rooms for out-of-town guests.
- \_\_\_\_ Choose wedding rings.
- \_\_\_\_ Send engagement announcement to newspapers.
- \_\_\_\_ Select and order wedding gown, leaving ample time for delivery and alterations.
- \_\_\_\_ Look for alteration specialist (if some- one other than bridal shop).
- \_\_\_\_ Finalize the attendants (bridesmaids and groomsmen). Choose and order bridesmaids dresses.
- \_\_\_\_ Purchase invitations.
- \_\_\_\_ Select one usher for every 50 guests.
- \_\_\_\_ Schedule wedding cake design appointment. Get estimates. Book the date.
- \_\_\_\_ Implement diet and exercise program.
- \_\_\_\_ Plan beauty preparations by checking with your salon for how far in advance they book wedding parties.
- \_\_\_\_ Finalize all honeymoon plans. If traveling outside the country, check on visas, passports and inoculations.
- \_\_\_\_ Sign up for dance lessons. Talk to instructor about choreographing a special dance routine to "wow" guests.
- \_\_\_\_ Book vendors, securing dates by putting down deposit.

## Four months or more before:

_____ Confirm final details with the caterer.
_____ Order napkins and purchase any other items needed for the ceremony and reception. Check with the caterer to see what he/she includes.
_____ Order invitations (25 extra) and personal stationery or "Thank You" notes.
_____ Book engagement photo session with enough time to submit photos to local newspapers.
_____ Visit the photographer again to discuss specifics. Use the "Photography Worksheet."
_____ Get estimates and order flowers and floral arrangements for wedding and reception.
_____ Get estimates and order balloons, decorations and favors for wedding and reception.
_____ Book room for wedding night.

## Three months or more before:

_____ Order wedding rings. Allow time for any final engraving.
_____ Order tuxedos for the groomsmen and fathers.

## Two months or more before:

_____ Mail invitations (six weeks before the wedding; eight weeks to out-of-town guests).
_____ Buy a wedding gift for future spouse and gifts for attendants and helpers.
_____ Finalize arrangements of accommodations for out-of-town attendants and guests.

## One month or more before:

_____ Ready all accessories, shoes and lingerie for bridal gown.

_____ Have beauty consultant do a trial run with bride's hair and makeup. Schedule this appointment on the day the bridal portrait is taken and/or a party is planned or schedule on the day of your final dress fitting to see exactly how you will look on wedding day.

_____ Have final fitting for bridal gown and bridesmaids' dresses.

_____ Have bridal portrait taken.

_____ Have groomsmen registered and measured at the formal wear store.

_____ Check with the newspapers on wedding announcement requirements.

_____ Finalize plans for rehearsal dinner.

_____ Plan seating arrangements for the rehearsal dinner and reception.

_____ Review this checklist to be sure nothing has been missed.

_____ Complete change-of-address information for post-office.

_____ Keep current with "Thank You" notes for shower and early wedding gifts.

## Two weeks before:

_____ Get the marriage license. Be sure to bring all needed documents.

_____ Inform or send rehearsal invitations including exact time and location to those who will attend the rehearsal and rehearsal dinner.

_____ Inquire about where bride, groom and attendants will dress for the ceremony.

_____ Review all details. Walk through the entire event considering things like parking, access for handicapped guests, etc.

_____ Confirm all transportation plans.

_____ Check in with caterer, photographer, videographer, musicians, DJ, florist, etc. to confirm all arrangements.

_____ "Break in" wedding shoes at home.

## One week before:

\_\_\_\_ Appoint someone to act as an "organizer" to handle any last minute problems.
\_\_\_\_ Give a final guest count to the caterer.
\_\_\_\_ Review final details for those in the wedding party.
\_\_\_\_ Confirm honeymoon arrangements.
\_\_\_\_ Pack for the honeymoon.
\_\_\_\_ Enjoy a day with family and friends. Visit a day spa, have a massage, a facial and relax.

## One day before:

\_\_\_\_ Attend the rehearsal and rehearsal dinner and give gifts to attendants.
\_\_\_\_ Give the rings and clergy's fee to the best man.
\_\_\_\_ Organize gown, accessories, etc. to go to ceremony.
\_\_\_\_ Get a manicure and pedicure.

## On the wedding day:

\_\_\_\_ Mail wedding announcements.
\_\_\_\_ Get hair, makeup, etc. done.
\_\_\_\_ Enjoy the day!

Electronic versions of this tool with room for notes are available upon request at **products@newbizplaybook.com**

# Venue Checklist

This checklist is to be used for interviewing venues, and tracking their answers to insure that they are a good fit for the client's needs. It is always a good idea to tour the venue early where economics permit, to see for yourself if the place is as nice as the well situated online pictures make it appear to be. When a venue impresses you, be sure to document that, and keep it mind. Relationships with quality reliable vendors are absolutely essential to success in this business.

Capacity

    \_\_\_\_ Reception Area
    \_\_\_\_ Theatre/Meeting Room
    \_\_\_\_ Dining Area

Caterer

    \_\_\_\_ Exclusive caterers?
    \_\_\_\_ In-house tables/linens/chairs? If so, check out the quality.
    \_\_\_\_ Typical menu cost per head for cocktails, heavy appetizers, etc.
    \_\_\_\_ Bar tender charges?
    \_\_\_\_ Serving Charges?
    \_\_\_\_ Cake cutting charges?
    \_\_\_\_ Minimum food and beverage spend?
    \_\_\_\_ How early can your caterer arrive day of event to set up?

Rental Fees

    \_\_\_\_ Usually negotiable, especially for a major brand/off day
    \_\_\_\_ Does fee include a set up day?

- ___ How early/late can your teams load in?
- ___ Any discount for payment by check or early payment?
- ___ Hotels should waive any room rentals when F&B meets a min.

## Bathrooms

- ___ Will you need to provide extra amenities to make the room nicer
- ___ Cleanliness – poorly kept restrooms reflect poorly managed venue
- ___ Number of stalls vs. number of guests

## Parking

- ___ Existent?
- ___ Fee to use parking lot?
- ___ Valets – included? Is there a preferred valet company?
- ___ Buses – if using buses - is there room to turn around, unload?

## Shipments

- ___ Will the venue accept and store boxes a few days before event? $?

## Audiovisual Team

- ___ Exclusive AV Company?
- ___ What tech operators are included, if any? (lighting tech, sound, camera)
- ___ Cost of in-house AV Team/hour/operator

\_\_\_\_ What AV exists in house? See the quality of the projector and check compatibility.
\_\_\_\_ Internet Access- speed and logistics (do you need to drop lines, $$$)
\_\_\_\_ Cost to use existing Internet lines

## Stages

\_\_\_\_ Note any restrictions and size dimensions
\_\_\_\_ Height from ground to hang points
\_\_\_\_ See stage lighting with the room dark
\_\_\_\_ Existing backdrops, can you utilize these for event?
\_\_\_\_ If a stage must be brought in understand load-in logistics/restrictions

## Registration/Place card area

\_\_\_\_ Is there a clean, open space near entrance of venue and in front of main room?
\_\_\_\_ How much signage can be placed outside of meeting room, in common areas?
\_\_\_\_ Will other events be held during meeting/wedding/party?
\_\_\_\_ Does venue have staff to help with registration/guiding guests to room?

## Entrance

\_\_\_\_ Opportunity to brand/decorate entrance area?
\_\_\_\_ Curb appeal; are you comfortable with the current look/feel of the entrance?

Reception Area

    \_\_\_\_ How close is the area to the ceremony/meeting room?
    \_\_\_\_ Ideally a large open space with the ability to brand/decorate
    \_\_\_\_ What furniture can be utilized for event?
    \_\_\_\_ Will venue take away existing furniture you don't want for your event?

Any charges?

    \_\_\_\_ How early can you set up in this area?

Other Clients

    \_\_\_\_ Who else has held events at this venue in recent months?
    \_\_\_\_ Testimonials? Can you contact references?
    \_\_\_\_ Has a major competitor hosted parties at this venue for a similar client base?

Electronic versions of this tool with room for notes are available upon request at **products@newbizplaybook.com**.

# Marketing for Event Planners

Of all the challenges a new event planner faces, marketing the business can feel the most overwhelming. The good news is that you can very easily, and inexpensively market your business to a receptive target audience. The challenge will be follow through and consistency in maintaining exposure for your brand.

Whole books have been written on the subject of marketing, and this material is not designed to replace them. Our hope is to provide you with guidance as to how to spend your time, and where. You should understand the pros and cons of the various options out there, to make intelligent decisions on your ROI or return on investment. Everyone has different results with different media. As important as this is to your success, you should track where your leads (especially the ones that hire you), are coming from. Advertising that appears expensive at the outset, maybe cheap relative to other options when you see the revenue it is generating.

**Website/SEO**
Your website if properly done can be a very useful marketing tool, and may be one of the places you spend early money, once you start getting gigs. Wordpress.org, has some incredibly easy templated websites that can get you started. If you can get to a place where you are on the first or second page of google with your site, which is very doable, this will be the single most effective marketing vehicle you have. Keep in mind, you aren't looking to be first when someone types "wedding planner." You are looking to be first when someone type "wedding planner in Cleveland." The difference between these two is what makes it vastly easier to rise to the top. I have, with no training whatsoever, been able to get several service based websites on the first page of google.

The key is to duplicate the search you want to be relevant for. For example, if the hope is that you come up first when someone types "event planners in St. Louis," do that search, and then go to the sites on the first page and a half of google, and look at the content. You are specifically looking for whether there are videos or pictures, how often your key search term appears.

You are also looking for the titles used for the website's pages. For example if you click on a page, at the top right side of that page there will be a tab, with some language on it that is designed to summarize the content of that page. These are title tags, and this research on content, will tell you what you need to emulate to get to the top of google. Be careful. Copying text and directly duplicating material, or over using a few key words will get you punted from key word searches, which would kill the effectiveness of your website. When you start to book events, you should consider early investment in a great website with an SEO (search engine optimization) professional to help you.

We recommend that at a minimum, a third of all profits go back into the business to grow it and help with important investments in the business. This investment would be at the top of that list. If you have some resources already saved, this would boost visibility substantially and increase the speed with which your business gets noticed. There are a number of free-lance website development options out there. Do your research as this is a hugely important investment.

**Networking and Word of Mouth**

Experienced, successful event planners will tell you that most of their new business comes from referrals and relationships they have formed with clients, and others in the business such as wedding photographers, and other wedding service providers. The challenge is to reach the level where the "machine" is sending you leads on a constant basis. As you build relationships with these professionals, and help them to build their businesses, it is reasonable to expect that they help with yours. You should be candid in hiring these folks about what you are looking for. It is reasonable to demand promptness, professionalism, responsiveness, and elite service from these folks. Let them know that in your mind they are an extension of your brand, and if they provide an exceptional experience for your bride, you will help build their businesses. It is interesting to hear from new planners that they feel uncomfortable asking these folks for referrals. That is part of the job here

In the beginning you should be very vocal to your personal network of friends and family to let them know you have begun to do this work, being sure to emphasize all of your efforts, research, and time spent getting to know the business.

**Wedding Shows**

Wedding and Bridal Shows – Few venues will give you as much exposure to potential clients in such a short amount of time as Wedding shows.  They are also among the most expensive marketing options available to a new startup.  Prices for large city shows range from $1000 for a small booth to more than $1600 for a larger one.  These costs don't include expenses for any attention getting show pieces you may want to feature.  There will also be some competition among other planners vying for the business of the same clients in a relatively small setting.  – Tip If you are just starting out, and don't have a good portfolio of pictures of your work (which we will talk about getting inexpensively or free from photographers later), research designs you like online with sites like Pinterest and others and create a book of "ideas we love for your weeding."  Make sure these are things that you will be able to recreate with reasonable effort if asked to do so, but visualization is very important to getting clients to hire you.

**Social Media**

Social media is an incredibly effective and inexpensive means of advertising your business, and to a limited degree it is worth your time to learn how to get your brand up and running on Facebook, Instagram, twitter, Pinterest, and snapchat. This is how you build a following, and stay relevant to others who need to think of you first when they or someone they know decides to get married. In the beginning these are free if not very inexpensive. Once you get traction, placing ads may make a huge difference. Next to Wedding Shows, this can be the most impactful marketing media available to you.

**Ratings and specialty sites**

There are a number of sites like Yelp, which allow businesses to put up very basic profiles for free. In the beginning, it can be helpful to put your site and business on as many of these as possible so that these sites point back to your website and business. When you sign up, you will be pitched on pay packages that help boost your chances of appearing early on these sites. In our experience these types of investment don't generate nearly as many live leads as search engine optimization. It is important to monitor these sites, and to regularly search for your site so that you can see what reviews are out there both good and bad, which could impact your business.

**Phone books, mailers and other print advertising**

We address these last, because frankly they are not very effective in generating revenue relative to the cost, at least in this business. At some point, you may be large enough to require a better add in a phone book, or need to have mail outs for clients to stay in front of them, but getting email addresses, and electronic communication is vastly more effective. We simply don't recommend spending startup dollars here.

You may have need for printed material in the form of business cards or trifolds, which can be handed out to guests who visit you at wedding shows etc. These are necessary expenditures, and when they are printed it should be high quality work on good card or paper stock. This stuff represents your brand, which must be elite if you want to command larger fees with your engagements.

We have included a great example of a tri fold in word form, so you don't have to play with formatting or make one yourself. Simply cut and paste photos or logos and add content as you see fit. Below is a printed example with two sides of a suggested layout, with content references that will allow you adjust the tri-fold to fit your business.

# Food and Beverage Planning

**Appetizers**

As you determine the appetizer quantity, consider what purpose the appetizers will serve. If you're serving appetizers before a main meal, you don't need as many as you do if the appetizers are the meal itself. Because appetizers are different from other food items, how much you need depends on several factors. Appetizers don't lend themselves to a quantity chart, per se, but let the following list guide you:

- For appetizers preceding a full meal, you should have at least four different types of appetizers and six to eight pieces (total) per person. For example, say you have 20 guests. In that case, you'd need at least 120 total appetizer pieces.

- For appetizers without a meal, you should have at least six different types of appetizers. You should also have 12 to 15 pieces (total) per person. For example, if you have 20 guests, you need at least 240 total appetizer pieces. This estimate is for a three-hour party. Longer parties require more appetizers.

- The more variety you have, the smaller portion size each type of appetizer will need to have. Therefore, you don't need to make as much of any one particular appetizer.

- When you serve appetizers to a crowd, always include bulk-type appetizers. Bulk-type foods are items that aren't individually made, such as dips or spreads. If you forgo the dips and spreads, you'll end up making hundreds of individual appetizer items, which may push you over the edge. To calculate bulk items, assume 1 ounce equals 1 piece.

- Always try to have extra items, such as black and green olives and nuts, for extra filler.

When appetizers precede the meal, you should serve dinner within an hour. If more than an hour will pass before the meal, then you need to increase the number of appetizers. Once again, always err on the side of having too much rather than too little.

**Quantity planning for soups, sides, main courses, and desserts**

The following tables can help you determine how much food you need for some typical soups, sides, main courses, and desserts. If the item you're serving isn't listed here, you can probably find an item in the same food group to guide you.

You may notice a bit of a discrepancy between the serving per person and the crowd servings. The per-person serving is based on a plated affair (where someone else has placed the food on the plates and the plates are served to the guests). In contrast, buffet-style affairs typically figure at a lower serving per person because buffets typically feature more side dish items than a plated meal does. Don't use the quantity tables as an exact science; use them to guide you and help you make decisions for your particular crowd. If you're serving a dish that you know everyone loves, then make more than the table suggests. If you have a dish that isn't as popular, you can get by with less.

## Soups and Stews

| Soup or Stew | Per Person | Crowd of 25 | Crowd of 50 |
| --- | --- | --- | --- |
| Served as a first course | 1 cup | 5 quarts | 2-1/2 gallons |
| Served as an entree | 1-1/2 to 2 cups | 2 to 2-1/2 gallons | 4 gallons |

## Main Courses

| Entree | Per Person | Crowd of 25 | Crowd of 50 |
| --- | --- | --- | --- |
| Baby-back ribs, pork spareribs, beef short ribs | 1 pound | 25 pounds | 50 pounds |
| Casserole | N/A | Two or three 9-x-13-inch casseroles | Four or five 9-x-13-inch casseroles |
| Chicken, turkey, or duck (boneless) | 1/2 pound | 13 pounds | 25 pounds |
| Chicken or turkey (with bones) | 3/4 to 1 pound | 19 pounds | 38 pounds |
| Chili, stew, stroganoff, and other chopped meats | 5 to 6 ounces | 8 pounds | 15 pounds |

| | | | |
|---|---|---|---|
| Ground beef | 1/2 pound | 13 pounds | 25 pounds |
| Maine lobster (about 2 lbs. each) | 1 | 25 | 50 |
| Oysters, clams, and mussels (medium to large) | 6 to 10 pieces | 100 to 160 pieces | 200 to 260 pieces |
| Pasta | 4 to 5 ounces | 7 pounds | 16 pounds |
| Pork | 14 ounces | 22 pounds | 44 pounds |
| Roast (with bone) | 14 to 16 ounces | 22 to 25 pounds | 47 to 50 pounds |
| Roast cuts (boneless) | 1/2 pound | 13 pounds | 25 pounds |
| Shrimp (large: 16 to 20 per pound) | 5 to 7 shrimp | 7 pounds | 14 pounds |
| Steak cuts (T-bone, porterhouse, rib-eye) | 16 to 24 ounces | 16 to 24 ounces per person | 16 to 24 ounces per person |
| Turkey (whole) | 1 pound | 25 pounds | 50 pounds |

## Side Dishes

| *Side Dish* | *Per Person* | *Crowd of 25* | *Crowd of 50* |
|---|---|---|---|

| Ingredient | Per Person | Crowd of 25 | Crowd of 50 |
|---|---|---|---|
| Asparagus, carrots, cauliflower, broccoli, green beans, corn kernels, peas, black-eyed peas, and so on | 3 to 4 ounces | 4 pounds | 8 pounds |
| Corn on the cob (broken in halves when serving buffet-style) | 1 ear | 20 ears | 45 ears |
| Pasta (cooked) | 2 to 3 ounces | 3-1/2 pounds | 7 pounds |
| Potatoes and yams | 1 (medium) | 6 pounds | 12 pounds |
| Rice and grains (cooked) | 1-1/2 ounces | 2-1/2 pounds | 5 pounds |

## Side Salads

| Ingredient | Per Person | Crowd of 25 | Crowd of 50 |
|---|---|---|---|
| Croutons (medium size) | N/A | 2 cups | 4 cups |
| Dressing (served on the side) | N/A | 4 cups | 8 cups |
| Fruit salad | N/A | 3 quarts | 6 quarts |
| Lettuce (iceberg or romaine) | N/A | 4 heads | 8 heads |
| Lettuce (butter or red leaf) | N/A | 6 heads | 12 heads |

| | | | |
|---|---|---|---|
| Potato or macaroni salad | N/A | 8 pounds | 16 pounds |
| Shredded cabbage for coleslaw | N/A | 6 to 8 cups (about 1 large head of cabbage) | 12 to 16 cups (about 2 large heads of cabbage) |
| Vegetables (such as tomato and cucumber) | N/A | 3 cups | 6 cups |

## Breads

| Bread | Per Person | Crowd of 25 | Crowd of 50 |
|---|---|---|---|
| Croissants or muffins | 1-1/2 per person | 3-1/2 dozen | 7 dozen |
| Dinner rolls | 1-1/2 per person | 3-1/2 dozen | 7 dozen |
| French or Italian bread | N/A | Two 18-inch loaves | Four 18-inch loaves |

## Desserts

| Dessert | Per Person | Crowd of 25 | Crowd of 50 |
|---|---|---|---|
| Brownies or bars | 1 to 2 per person | 2-1/2 to 3 dozen | 5-1/2 to 6 dozen |
| Cheesecake | 2-inch | Two 9-inch | Four 9-inch |

|  |  | wedge | cheesecakes | cheesecakes |
| --- | --- | --- | --- | --- |
| Cobbler |  | 1 cup | Two 9-x-9-x-2-inch pans | Four 9-x-9-x-2-inch pans |
| Cookies |  | 2 to 3 | 3 to 4 dozen | 6 to 8 dozen |
| Ice cream or sorbet |  | 8 ounces | 1 gallon | 2 gallons |
| Layered cake or angel food cake |  | 1 slice | Two 8-inch cakes | Four 8-inch cakes |
| Pie |  | 3-inch wedge | Two or three 9-inch pies | Four or five 9-inch pies |
| Pudding, trifles, custards, and the like |  | 1 cup | 1 gallon | 2 gallons |
| Sheet cake |  | 2-x-2-inch piece | 1/4 sheet cake | 1/2 sheet cake |

## Alcohol and Beverage Planning

Concerning drinks, let the following list guide you:

> Soft drinks: One to two 8-ounce servings per person per hour.
>
> Punch: One to two 4-ounce servings per person per hour.
>
> Tea: One to two 8-ounce servings per person per hour.
>
> Coffee: One to two 4-ounce servings per person per hour.
>
> Water: Always provide it. Two standard serving pitchers per table are usually enough.
>
> Again, err on the side of having too much. If people are eating a lot and having fun, they tend to consume more liquid.

## Alcohol Consumption and Pricing Projection Tool

There is always some subjectivity in alcohol planning. The assumption here is that 75% of the guests are drinking alcohol. This should be discussed, as a higher percentage of children in attendance, a group of heavier drinkers etc., could impact these assumptions.

As always we recommend adding 10% to all estimates. You will frustrate guests if there is insufficient alcohol, so make sure they are in agreement with your assumptions on numbers. They will know their guests better than anyone. The cost estimates assume average costs on beer, wine, and liquor. Premium beer, wine, and liquor would also mean increased costs. This also assumes equal consumption i.e. 25% each of beer, wine, and liquor. Beer drinkers tend to range closer to 40%, but these figures make scaling for your needs much easier.

The following should help plan for reception alcohol consumption.
BD = beer drinker, WD = wine drinker, LD = liquor drinker

|  | Small Wedding (100 guests) | |
|---|---|---|
|  | Amount | Cost |
| Beer | 5 cases per 25 BD | 75.00 |
| Wine | 20 bottles per 25 WD | 160.00 |
| Liquor | 6 750 ml bottles per 25 LD | 90.00 |

|  | Medium Wedding (200 guests) | |
|---|---|---|
|  | Amount | Cost |
| Beer | 9 cases per 50 BD | 135.00 |
| Wine | 40 bottles per 50 WD | 320.00 |
| Liquor | 12 750 ml bottles per 50 LD | 180.00 |

|  | Large Wedding (100) | |
|---|---|---|
|  | Amount | Cost |
| Beer | 3 Kegs 100 BD | 270.00 |
| Wine | 79 bottles per 100 WD | 632.00 |
| Liquor | 24 750 ml bottles per 100 LD | 360.00 |

## Wedding Budget Tool

In the attachments, we have included an excel spreadsheet complete with all formulas and entries needed for a great wedding budget tool. You can add items, or leave 0's in emails that don't apply. This tool will help you and your clients plan costs, and adjust in real time for increased costs or savings to allow the necessary flexibility.

The below is a print version you can complete as needed, electronic spreadsheet available at products@newbizplaybook.com

| | |
|---|---|
| Total Budgeted Amount | |
| Guest Headcount (you can change this to see the figures below adjust) | |
| | |
| **Ceremony** | |
| Gown & Alterations | |
| Veil & Headpiece | |
| Bride's Accessories (lingerie, shoes, gloves, etc.) | |
| Bride's Hair & Makeup | |
| Bridesmaids Hair | |
| Bridesmaids wraps & purses | |
| Groomens Ties | |
| Site Fee | |
| Ceremony AV | |
| Officiant's Fee | |
| License and copies (4 @ $15 each) | |
| Accessories (arch, runner, etc.) | |
| | |
| **Hotel** | |
| Valet or Parking | |
| Food & Services ($X/Guest) | |
| Beverages & Bartenders ($40.00/Guest) | |
| Wedding Cake | |
| Recpetion Set up fees/dance floor | |
| Tax & Tip on food | |
| | |
| **Florals** | |
| Bridal Bouquet | |
| Flowers For Bride's Attendants ($60/Bride Attendant) | |
| Flowers For Groom's Attendants ($25/Groom Attendant) | |
| Other florals for guests | |
| tax on flowers | |

| | |
|---|---|
| Reception Centerpieces & Decor ($80 each*12) | |
| | |
| **Children** | |
| Child Care | |
| TV Rental | |
| Children's Meals | |
| | |
| **Entertainment** | |
| Ceremony Musician | |
| Reception Band | |
| Photographer | |
| Videographer | |
| | |
| **Guests** | |
| Shuttle Rental ($150/first run, $100 additional) | |
| Bride & Groom's Hotel Rooms | |
| Attendant Gifts ($x/Attendant) | |
| Donation/Favors ($x/Guest) | |
| Welcome Baskets ($x ea.) | |
| | |

| | |
|---|---|
| **Printed Materials** | |
| Invitations (reply cards, calligraphy, postage, etc.) | |
| Other Stationery (programs, thank you notes) | |
| Menu cards | |
| Welcome Party Invites/Rehearsal Dinner Invites | |
| | |
| TOTAL: | |
| | |

| Festivities around Wedding: | |
|---|---|
| (often these are covered by a parent or a separate budget) | |
| Bridesmaids Brunch | |
| | Tax/Tip 28% |
| | |
| Groomsmen Golf Outing | |
| Food on course | |
| | |
| Welcome Party | |
| food | |
| Alcohol | |

| | Tax |
|---|---|
| | |
| Rehearsal Dinner | |
| food | |
| alcohol | |
| Reception hall rental | |
| equipment rental (margarita machines lights etc.) | |
| silverware rental/ linen costs/plate & crystal costs | |
| waitstaff/bartenders | |
| decorations | |
| fun photo booth etc. | |
| Tip/Tax | Tax/Tip 28% |
| | |
| **Total Wedding Festivities:** | |

Electronic versions of this spreadsheet are available upon request at **products@newbizplaybook.com**.

# Linen Planning Tool

| TABLE SIZE | SEATS | 54" Sq | 80" Sq | 90" Sq | 72x120" | 70x170" | 90x132" | 90x156" | 96" Rnd | 108" Rnd | 120" Rnd | 126" Rnd | 132" Rnd |
|---|---|---|---|---|---|---|---|---|---|---|---|---|---|
| 4'x3' | 4 | Overlay | 16x23" Drop | | | | | | | | | | |
| 6'x3' | 6–8 | | | Overlay | 24x21" Drop | Box | | | Overlay, Pinned | Overlay, Pinned | Overlay, Pinned | | |
| 8'x3' | 8–10 | | | Overlay | 12x21" Drop | Box | | | Overlay, Pinned | Overlay, Pinned | Overlay, Pinned | | |
| 6'x18" | 3 (One Side) | | | | 24x27" Drop | Box | | To Floor All Sides | | | | | |
| 8'x18" | 4 (One Side) | | | | 12x27" Drop | Box | To Floor All Sides | | | | | | |
| 30"x30" | 4 | 12" Drop* | 25" Drop* | To Floor All Sides | | | | | | | | | |

44 NEWBIZPLAYBOOK

# Linen Planning Tool

| TABLE SIZE | SEATS | 54" Sq | 80" Sq. | 90" Sq | 72x120" | 70x120" | 90x132" | 90x156" | 96" Rnd. | 108" Rnd. | 120" Rnd | 126" Rnd | 132" Rnd |
|---|---|---|---|---|---|---|---|---|---|---|---|---|---|
| 30" Round | 3 | Overlay 12" Drop | | | | | | | To Floor | | | | |
| 3' Round | 4 | Overlay 9" Drop | Overlay 22" Drop | | | | | | To Floor | | | | |
| Cafe Tables | Standing | Overlay 9" Drop | Overlay 22" Drop | Overlay 27" Drop | | | | | Overlay 30" Drop | To Floor | | | |
| 4' Round | 6 | Overlay Top | Overlay 16" Drop | Overlay 21" Drop | | | | | Overlay 24" Drop | To Floor | | | |
| 5' Round | 8–10 | | Overlay 10" Drop | Overlay 15" Drop | | | | | Overlay 18" Drop | Overlay 24" Drop | To Floor | | |
| 5½' Round | 9–10 | | Overlay 7" Drop | Overlay 12" Drop | | | | | Overlay 15" Drop | Overlay 21" Drop | 27" Drop | To Floor | |
| 6' Round | 10-12 | | Overlay Top | Overlay 9" Drop | | | | | Overlay 12" Drop | Overlay 18" Drop | 24" Drop | 27" Drop | To Floor |
| 1/2 Round | | | | | | | | | | | 1 Cloth, Folded | | |
| Serpentine | Buffet | 3 Cloths with 2 Skirts | | | 1 Cloth with 2 Skirts | 1 Cloth | | | | | | | |

# Seating Planning Tool

## Banquet Table

| Table Size | Seating Capacity | Linen Size | Space Needed |
|---|---|---|---|
| 6' | 6-8 | 90" x 132" | 11" x 7" |
| 8' | 8-10 | 90" x 156" | 13' x 7' |
| Classroom 6' | 4 | 70" x 170" | 11' x 6' |
| Classroom 8' | 6 | 70" x 170" | 13' x 6' |

## Round Table

| Table Size | Seating Capacity | Linen Size | Space Needed |
|---|---|---|---|
| 2.5' | 2-4 | 96" round | 7' diameter |
| 3' | 4-5 | 96" round | 8' diameter |
| 4' | 6-8 | 108" round | 9' diameter |
| 5' | 8-10 | 120" round | 10' diameter |
| 6' | 10-12 | 132" round | 11' diameter |

## Cocktail Table

| Table Size | Seating Capacity | Linen Size | Space Needed |
|---|---|---|---|
| 2.5' | 2-4 | 108" round | 7' diameter |
| 3' | 4-5 | 120" round | 8' diameter |

# Reception Planner Contact Tool

**Wedding Details**

Wedding Date _____

Client Contact Name _____

Phone _____ email _____

Client Address _____

City _____ Zip _____

Wedding Venue Name _____

Rec Venue Name _____

Wedding Venue Address _____

City _____ Zip _____

Rec Venue Address _____

City _____ Zip _____

Photographer _____

Photographer Phone _____

Videographer _____

Videographer Phone _____

Caterer          _____

Caterer Phone    _____

Electronic versions of this spreadsheet are available upon request at products@newbizplaybook.com.

# Wedding Party Contact Tool

Bride & Groom _____     Flower Girl _____

Bride Parents _____     Ring Bearer _____

Groom Parents _____     Minister _____

Made of Honor _____     Best Man _____

Gparents Bride _____    Gparents Groom _____

| Groom's Men | Brides Maids |
|---|---|
| 1. _____ | 1. _____ |
| 2. _____ | 2. _____ |
| 3. _____ | 3. _____ |
| 4. _____ | 4. _____ |
| 5. _____ | 5. _____ |
| 6. _____ | 6. _____ |
| 7. _____ | 7. _____ |
| 8. _____ | 8. _____ |

## Ushers

1._____    5._____

2._____    6._____

3._____    7._____

4._____    8._____

Events

Prayer/Grace _____    Toast Best Man _____

Father Bride Toast _____    Father Groom Toast _____

Dad Daughter Dance (song) _____

Mom Groom Dance (song) _____

Bride and Groom 1st Dance _____

Wedding Party (song) _____

Cake   Cutting   (song)   _____

Bouquet Toss (song) _____

Garter (song) _____

Special Requests _____

Groom Comments _____
Bride Comments _____

Special Requests _____

DJ musical genre preference _____

DJ style preference (active vs. camouflage)

## Order of Events (please number 1-15)

| Introduction | Toast | Father Daughter |
|---|---|---|
| Blessing | First Dance | Mother Groom |
| Bouquet Toss | Last Dance | Cake Cutting |
| Garter Toss | Other | Other |
| Other | Other | Other |

## Dinner Music or Special Songs

1. _____  2. _____

3. _____  4. _____

5. _____  6. _____

7. _____  8. _____

9. _____  10. _____

11. _____  12. _____

Electronic versions of this spreadsheet are available upon request at **products@newbizplaybook.com**.

## Dance Floor Planning Tool

This tool has been designed to allow you to plan and scale necessary floor space for dancing. For parties greater than 250, simply use multiples of the tables below. If more than 50% of guests are expected to be dancing, ignore the guests invited column, and plan based upon the number of dancers in the second column.

| Total Guests | Dancers | Dance FL Size | Floor SQ Feet |
| --- | --- | --- | --- |
| 24 | 12 | 8'x8' | 64 |
| 36 | 18 | 8'x12' | 96 |
| 48 | 24 | 8'x16' | 128 |
| 64 | 32 | 12'x12' | 144 |
| 72 | 36 | 12'x16' | 192 |
| 90 | 45 | 12'x20 | 240 |
| 96 | 48 | 16'x16' | 256 |
| 120 | 60 | 16'x24' | 384 |
| 128 | 64 | 16'x24' | 384 |
| 144 | 72 | 16'x24' | 384 |
| 150 | 75 | 20'x20' | 400 |
| 168 | 84 | 16'x28' | 448 |
| 180 | 90 | 20'x24' | 480 |
| 192 | 96 | 16'x32' | 512 |
| 210 | 105 | 20'x28' | 560 |
| 250 | 125 | 24'x28' | 672 |

## Guest List Management Tool

This tool is most easily used in spreadsheet form. An excel file tool is available at newbizplaybook.com. For those who want to download it.

With proper planning, a fair amount of information is needed on each guest including:

1. First and last name

2. Telephone number

3. Address and/or email address

4. Invitation sent

5. Confirmed for attending wedding/or not

6. Confirmed for attending pre-wedding dinner/or not – out of town guests for example

7. Wedding gift

8. Thank you letter sent

Download a great tool for helping the bride and groom keep track of attendance, and their responsibilities for thank you cards etc. This tool also helps the event planner to track and make adjustments for food, dance etc., in the event that more or fewer guests attend than expected. Electronic versions of this spreadsheet will be sent to readers upon request at **products@newbizplaybook.com**.

# Important People Contact List

This tool is related, but different. Wedding and event planners need to have visibility, and to some degree information about the VIP guests. Whoever is hiring you to plan their event wants the people dearest to them to enjoy it as much as possible. For you to build that robust referral network that will grow your business, you need to see to these folks.

For the VIP guests, you will want to know:

1. Full name

2. Relationship to the client

3. Cell phone if assisting with arrangements

4. Flight information if planner will be assisting with transportation (arrivals departures etc.)

5. Hotel details

6. Notes if needed.

We have a spreadsheet tool that will help to track these issues at **products@newbizplaybook.com**.

# Packing Planning Tool

As silly as it sounds, one of the most common "emergencies," that plague weddings and events is forgotten items, missing clothing, or lost guest books etc. We have a spreadsheet tool to track these issues at **products@newbizplaybook.com**.

| General Items | Box Number | Location for Wedding | Goes home with... |
|---|---|---|---|
| *Pre-Ceremony Bride* | | | |
| Dress/Suit | freestanding | Hotel Room | Sara Smith |
| Headpeice | freestanding | Hotel Room | Sara Smith |
| Jewelry | freestanding | Hotel Room | Mrs. Bride's Mom |
| Ring | freestanding | Hotel Room | Bride |
| Shoes | freestanding | Hotel Room | Sara Smith |
| Suitcase | freestanding | Hotel Room | Sara Smith |
| Wedding Party Gifts | 1 | Parents House | Mrs. Groom's Mom |
| *Pre-Ceremony Groom* | | | |
| Tux | freestanding | Hotel Room | Joe Jones |
| Jewelry | freestanding | Hotel Room | Groom |
| Shoes | freestanding | Hotel Room | Joe Jones |
| Tie, cuff links, etc | freestanding | Hotel Room | Joe Jones |
| Ring | freestanding | Hotel Room | Groom |
| Suitcase | freestanding | Hotel Room | Mrs. Groom's Mom |
| Wedding Party Gifts | 3 | Parents House | Mrs. Groom's Mom |
| *Ceremony* | | | |
| Flowers | freestanding | B Parents House | Given to guests |
| Decorations | 4 | B Parents House | Given to guests |
| Wedding signs | freestanding | Parents House | Mrs. Bride's Mom |
| *Pre-Reception Bride* | | | |
| Rec Dress | freestanding | Hotel Room | Sara Smith |
| Jewelry | freestanding | Hotel Room | Bride |
| Shoes | freestanding | Hotel Room | Sara Smith |
| *Reception* | | | |
| Cake Cutter for guests | 1 | Parents House | Planner |
| Glue, Scissors, Pens, | 1 | Parents House | Planner |
| Escort Cards | 2 | B Parents House | Planner |
| Escort Card Board | freestanding | G Parents House | Planner |
| Guest book, | 2 | gParents House | Planner |
| Garters | 2 | Parents House | Planner |
| Cake Knife For Pictures | 2 | Parents House | Planner |
| Kids Table Kits | 2 | Parents House | Planner |
| *Etc.* | | | |
| CPR Paddles | 1 | Church/Venue | |
| Parking Lot Signs | freestanding | Venue | Planner |
| Sewing Kit | 1 | Church/Venue | Planner |
| Deodorant/ etc | 1 | Church/Venue | Planner |
| Hair pins/ supply | 1 | Church/Venue | Planner |
| Emergency Kit | 1 | Church/Venue | Planner |
| Step stool | freestanding | Church/Venue | Planner |

# Vendor Contact Planning Sheet

| Vendor | Business Name | Contact Name | Contact Number | Payment Status |
|---|---|---|---|---|
| Photographer | | | | |
| Minister/Rabi | | | | |
| Bakery | | | | |
| Bar Tenders | | | | |
| Wait staff | | | | |
| Caterer | | | | |
| Videographer | | | | |
| D.J. | | | | |
| Flowers | | | | |

# Vendor Commitment Sheet

| Vendor | Commitment | Arrival Time | Notes - | Gets Meal - |
|---|---|---|---|---|
| Photographer | 8 hours x2 | | | |
| Minister/Rabi | | | | |
| Bakery | | 2.pm | | |
| Bar Tenders | | | | |
| Wait staff | | | | No |
| Caterer | | | | |
| Videographer | | | | |
| D.J. | | | | |
| Flowers | | | | |

## Week of Wedding Schedule Tool

| Time | Event | Location | Responsible Organizer |
|---|---|---|---|
| 3:30 PM | Bride and Bridesmaids Arrive, | Bride's Apt | Maiden of Honor |
| 4:30 PM | Rehearsal | The Church | Couple, Wedding Party |
| 5:00 PM | Set up for Rehearsal Dinner | Groom's Parents' House | Groom, Groom's Parents |
| 5:00 PM | Caterer arrives; begins set-up | Groom's Parents' House | Caterer |
| 5:30 PM | Couple arrives | Groom's Parents' House | The Couple |
| 6:00 PM | Guests arrive | Groom's Parents' House | Everyone |
| 7:00 PM | Food served | Groom's Parents' House | Caterer |
| 8:15 PM | Caterer packs up | Groom's Parents' House | Caterer |
| 9:30 PM | Couple leaves | Groom's Parents' House | The Couple |
| 10:00 PM | Clean-up | Groom's Parents' House | Groom's Parents & volunteers |
| Begin at 7:30 AM | | *SEE DAY OF SPREADSHEET* | |
| 10:00 AM | Post Wedding Brunch | Acme Restaurant | Best Man and Maiden of Honor |

56  NEWBIZPLAYBOOK

Proper organization insures that everyone knows where to be and when. In many instances, there may be a need to add or remove events, change times, locations, or even responsible organizer. This tool allows everyone to be on the same page. The responsible organizer examples above are not intended to be a comment as to who should traditionally handle what. They are only present as an example. Electronic versions of this spreadsheet are available upon request at **products@newbizplaybook.com**.

# Day of Wedding Schedule Tool

| When | What | Where | Who |
|---|---|---|---|
| | Pre-Ceremony | | |
| 7:00 AM | Bride wakes up | Bride's Apt | Bride |
| 7:30 AM | Friends arrive to do hair & makeup | Bride's Apt | Bride + friends |
| 8:00 AM | pick up decorations | Wedding Planner Storage | Wedding Stage Manager |
| 8:15 AM | photographer arrives | Church | Photographer |
| 8:30 AM | Church opens | Church | Wedding Stage Manager |
| 8:30 AM | set up begins | Church | wedding party |
| 8:15 AM | Bride and Groom Leave for Church | Church | Couple |
| 8:45 AM | Photographer leaves for venue | Church | Photographer |
| 8:45 AM | sound system check | Church | Wedding Singer |
| 9:00 AM | Photographer arrives for photos | Church | Photographer + Couple |
| 9:15 AM | Family Arrives for photos | Church | Wedding Party & Family |
| 9:30 AM | Family Photos | Church | Photographer + Family + Couple |
| 9:30 AM | flowers set up at Chruch | Church | Florist |
| 9:50 AM | Wedding party photos | Church | Couple |
| 10:30 AM | Reception set up begins | Venue | wedding party |
| 11:30 AM | Final Wedding Touch ups Minister Arrives | Church | Minister and wedding party family |
| 11:45 AM | Usher's take their places and begin seating | Church | ushers |
| 12:15 PM | Guests are all seated and Wedding Party in Place | Church | all |
| 12:20 PM | Wedding Ceremony | Church | all |
| 1:00 PM | Couple + Wedding Party get ready | Getting Ready Area | Couple + Wedding Party |

58 NEWBIZPLAYBOOK

# Day of Wedding Schedule Tool

## Cocktail Hour

| Time | Event | Location | Who |
|---|---|---|---|
| 1:30 PM | Couple Quiet time | take a walk | couple |
| 1:55 PM | cocktail hour | venue | Wedding Stage Manager/ caterer |
| 2:00 PM | Couple Photos | venue | photog, couple |
| 2:15 PM | Couple joins party | venue | couple |

## Reception

| Time | Event | Location | Who |
|---|---|---|---|
| 10:00 AM | cake picked up from bakery | bakery address | Reception Manager |
| 2:30 PM | guest seated for brunch | venue | Wedding Stage Manager/ caterer |
| 3:00 PM | toasts - four total | dance floor | names of toast givers |
| 4:15 PM | meal over | venue | Wedding Stage Manager/ caterer |
| 5:00 PM | first dance | dance floor | couple |
| 5:35 PM | dance Bride and Dad Groom and Mom | dance floor | all |
| 6:00 PM | cake cutting | venue | Wedding Stage Manager cues |
| 6:05 PM | dance | dance floor | all |
| 11:30 PM | last call | venue | announced by Wedding Stage Manager |
| 11:45 PM | Send off | venue | Wedding Stage Manager cues |
| 12:00 PM | guests out | venue | Wedding Stage Manager cues |

## Post-Reception

| Time | Event | Location | Who |
|---|---|---|---|
| 5:00 PM | caterer & family start breakdown | venue | caterer/ family |
| 10-12:30 PM | families leave with stuff they're taking | venue | family |
| 1:00 AM | breakdown done, everyone out | venue | all |

These are only present as an example. Electronic versions of this spreadsheet are available upon request at **products@newbizplaybook.com**

## Invoice Template

Your invoice is as much a reflection of your brand as any business card. You want to finish your engagement as professionally as you started it. We have included a template, and an electronic copy is available at **products@newbizplaybook.com**. Your invoice should include all of the following:

**[Company Name]**
[Company slogan]

[Street Address]
[City, ST ZIP Code]
Phone [Phone] | Fax [Fax]
[Email] | [Website]

**TO**
[Name]
[Company Name]
[Street Address]
[City, ST ZIP Code]
Phone [Phone] | [Email]

# INVOICE

INVOICE # [Invoice No.]
DATE [Date]

FOR [Project or service description]
P.O. # [P.O. #]

| Description | Amount |
|---|---|
| | |

**Total**

Make all checks payable to [Company Name]
Payment is due within 30 days.
If you have any questions concerning this invoice, contact [Name] | [Phone] | [Email]

THANK YOU FOR YOUR BUSINESS!

# Photographer Interview Questions

Attached are some questions to ask when interviewing photographers, but prior to that, you should speak to your client about what they want in terms of wedding photography both in the deliverable, and with the style of photographer and his interaction with guests, and the wedding party. The photographer should be willing to answer these questions and this interview will give you a sense of his or her business temperament. Eventually you will have a stable of talented vendors who can help you here based on your specific needs, and you may develop special requests that help you make the events you handle unique. *You should also be prepared to provide the photographer with any needed information such as divorced guests, who do not wish to be photographed together etc.

1. Do you have my date available?

2. Do you have an online portfolio that I, and/or my client can review to get a sense of your style, and how recent is the material on it?

3. How far in advance do I need to book with you?

4. How long have you been in business/How many weddings have you shot?

5. Are there references you can offer from prior clients or planners? Note: This is the important question in the interview. Do not hire someone who cannot provide you this information, and call at least a couple of the references to compare their answers to your photographer's responses to these questions.

6. How would you describe your photography style (e.g. traditional, photojournalistic, and creative)?

7. How would you describe your approach to interacting with wedding party and guests, i.e. blending in, stirring the pot for creative photos, choreographing shots?

8. What type of equipment do you use?

9. Are you shooting in digital or film format or both?

10. Do you shoot in color and black & white?

11. Can I give you a list of specific shots we would like?

12. How will you (and your assistants) be dressed?

13. Is it okay if other people take photos while you're taking photos?

14. Have you ever shot at (wedding/reception venue)? If not, would you be willing to visit in advance to plan?

15. What time will you arrive at the site and for how long will you shoot?

16. If my event lasts longer than expected, will you stay? Is there an additional charge?

17. Can you put together a slideshow of the bride and groom with provided photos and/or a real time slide show for viewing at the reception?

18. What information do you need from me before the wedding day?

19. What is your rate, and how is ownership of the photos handled? Bride and groom may want to own the photos to copy and use as they see fit, and this may impact price.

20. Are you the photographer who will shoot my wedding? If not, who will shoot it, and can I see their work? If so, who will be assisting you and how?

21. What are your travel charges/requirements if any?

22. Are you photographing other events on the same day as this event?

23. What type of album designs do you offer? Do you provide any assistance in creating an album?

24. Do you provide retouching, color adjustment or other corrective services?

25. How long after the wedding will I get the proofs? Will they be viewable online? On a CD?

26. What is the ordering process?

27. How long after I order my photos/album will I get them?

28. Will you give me the negatives or the digital images, and is there a fee for that?

29. When will I receive a written contract?

30. What is your refund/cancellation policy? Do you have someone who covers your events in case of emergency or equipment failure?

## Florist Interview Questions

1. Do you have my date available?

2. Do you have an online portfolio that I, and/or my client can review to get a sense of your style, and how recent is the material on it?

3. How far in advance do I need to book with you?

4. How long have you been in business/How many weddings have you handled?

5. Are there references you can offer from prior clients or planners? Note: This is the important question in the interview. Do not hire someone who cannot provide you this information, and call at least a couple of the references to compare their answers to your photographer's responses to these questions.

6. Given the size of this wedding, flower preference, color scheme, and venue specifics for church and reception, what would you propose? Note: Do not lead with your budget. Advise that you are open and want to see the proposal for a few different packages, so that you can compare costs.

7. What time will you arrive at the site and how long will it take you to set up?

8. Who will be managing the setup?

9. Are you providing flowers for other events on the same day as this event?

10. Any rental fees for vases or decorations the florist is providing?

11. Any additional labor charges, taxes, or other fee?

12. When will I receive a written contract?

13. What is your refund/cancellation policy? Do you have someone who covers your events in case of emergency? Note: It is common to require a 50% down payment.

# Flower Options for Weddings

## Wedding

### Bride's Flowers
    Bride's bouquet
    Bride's floral crown or hair flowers

### Groom Flowers
    Groom's boutonniere
    Groomsmens' boutonnieres

## Wedding Party Flowers
    Bridesmaids' bouquets
    Flower girl's bouquet or basket of pedals
    Ring bearer's boutonniere
    Mother of the bride's corsage
    Mother of the groom's corsage
    Father of the bride's boutonniere
    Father of the groom's boutonniere
    Grandmothers' corsages
    Grandfathers' boutonnieres
    Officiant's boutonniere
    Ushers' boutonnieres

## Ceremony Flowers
    Entryway or welcome table arrangements
    Altar/chuppah arrangements
    Pew or chair arrangements
    Candles
    Aisle decorations
    Tossing petals for guests

**Reception Flowers**

    Reception tossing bouquet
    Cocktail table arrangements
    Bar arrangements
    Escort-card table arrangements
    Centerpieces
    Bride's and groom's chair decorations
    Buffet-table/food-station arrangements
    Lounge area arrangements
    Flowers for wedding cake
    Cake table arrangements
    Powder room decorations
    Getaway car arrangements

# DJ Reception Planning Tool

Agenda:

6:00 PM Guests Arrive.   Background music begins.   Specify Background Music _____

6:15 PM        Introduction of the Wedding Party. Do you want to have your DJ announce your initial entrance into the reception? If so who,

6:30 PM        Bride/Groom Arrive

6:45 PM        Cocktails:   Decide between Classical, Jazz, Traditional New Age, Classic Soft Rock, Contemporary Soft Rock, (Bach, Vivaldi, etc.), (Brubeck, Basie), (Sinatra, Martin, etc.), (Yanni, Enya), (Billy Joel, Elton John, etc.), (Jack Johnson, Jason Mraz, Colbie Caillat, etc.)

7:00 PM        The best man's toast is traditionally done immediately before dinner, but can be done at any time. Please let us know if the father of the bride, the groom, or anyone else wants to say a few short words of welcome.

7:15 PM        Blessing is traditionally done immediately after the toast, and before the dinner is served. If there is a blessing,

7:30           Dinner: Classical, Jazz, Traditional New Age, Classic Soft Rock, Contemporary Soft Rock, (Bach, Vivaldi, etc.), (Brubeck, Basie), (Sinatra, Martin, etc.), (Yanni, Enya), (Billy Joel, Elton John, etc.), (Jack Johnson, Jason Mraz, Colbie Caillat, etc.)

8:15 PM        Traditional Dances. The traditional first dances of the evening will open up the dance floor, after which your guests will be able to dance for the rest of the evening. Typically, you will want to wait until a time when most of your guests are almost through with dinner. Please check off the dances you would like to include, as well as indicating which songs you would like to use for them.

Bride and Groom First Dance Song Title: _____ Artist:_____

Bride/Father Song Title: _____ Artist: _____

Groom/Mother Song Title: _____ Artist: _____

Wedding Party Song Title: _____ Artist:_____

All members of wedding party will dance (parents optional). Some may invite all guests to join ½ way through the song to kick off the dancing. Dance Music Begins.

8:30PM         Cake Cutting. When will you be cutting the cake? Please circle one: As you enter Before Dinner After Dinner

               Do you want a special song played at this time? Title: _____Artist:_____
               Would you like us to announce the cake cutting? Yes No

9:00PM    Bouquet and Garter Toss. Typically, if a couple chooses to throw the bouquet and/or the garter, they will wait at least 30 minutes after the last Traditional Dance to do so. Background music is usually played while the DJ calls the girls out for the bouquet and if the groom will throw the garter, a fun song is usually played while it is being removed.

Bouquet Song Title: _____ Artist:_____

Garter Song Title:_____ Artist:_____

9:30PM    Dollar Dance. As with the bouquet and garter toss, the dollar dance usually happens at least 30 minutes after the last Traditional Dance or immediately after the bouquet and garter toss. The dollar dance is optional.

DJ Details

What style DJ do you want: Quiet (no interaction during dancing) Moderate (interaction only if necessary) Outgoing (lots of interaction)

Is it more important for you to hear your favorite music, or for your guests to be dancing? _____

How many crowd-involvement songs would you like played (Electric Slide, Duck Dance, Cha Cha Slide, Cupid Shuffle, Anniversary Dance, etc.)?

These questions asked of your client will help to frame the experience they can expect from their DJ.

## Other Event Planning Tools

When we put this book together, we received a ton of great feedback from planners all over the event community, and one of the first comments they had was, "Can you add a section for (Bar mitzvah, Quincinera, or other large events/conferences)?" The following tools were born of our desired interest in helping readers, and in hopes of helping to increase the flexibility of their service offerings.

# Bar/Bat Mitzvah Reception Tool

Contact Information

Client name:                    Phone/Email:

Bar (boy) / Bat (girl) *(circle one)* Mitzvah name:

Reception Date:                 Setup Start Time:

Entertainment Start Time:       End Time:

The following is a typical but optional sequence of events. The specifics should be coordinated with relevant venders such as caterers, and DJ's etc.

| Sequence | Time | Event |
| --- | --- | --- |
|  |  | Guests Arrive |
|  |  | Cocktail Hour |
|  |  | Main Reception Starts (guests join each other in main hall) |
|  |  | Family Entrance |
|  |  | Candle Lighting |
|  |  | Hora |
|  |  | Kiddush |
|  |  | Motzi |
|  |  | Toasts |
|  |  | Salad within 30 minutes of entrance |
|  |  | Guest of Honor/Parent Dance |
|  |  | Main Course |
|  |  | Host/Hostess Dance |
|  |  | Dessert |
|  |  | Open Dancing |
|  |  | Finale |

## Venue Information

There are other tools in this publication for helping you to interview, plan for, and qualify the venue for your event. Those may be used here, so for example, there is a guest tracker in the wedding section. You may want to use something different for this event, but that will work here.

Name/address of establishment:

Contact name:   Phone:

Primary room name/location:

Planning Logistics


Number of guests:        Children:


Day School Guest of Honor attends:        Hebrew School Guest of Honor attends:


Party Theme:


Number of courses to be served (including dessert):


Will the caterer be using the dance floor for a buffet during the cocktail hour?        During the main course?

## Contact Information for Other Party Professionals

|  | Name | Phone | email | Booked From_ to _ |
|---|---|---|---|---|
| Caterer | Grande Dining Cuisine | (123)456-789 | abc@def.com | 7-9:30 |
| Banquet Hall/Venue |  |  |  |  |
| Planner/Coordinator |  |  |  |  |
| Photographer |  |  |  |  |
| Videographer |  |  |  |  |
| Entertainer |  |  |  |  |

## Cocktail Hour Planning Tool

Is cocktail hour in same room as main reception?    If not, what room is it in?

Music for cocktail hour:
Reception Start (Guests enter main reception room from cocktail room)

Music to start with (high-energy dance music recommended):

Reception Grand Entrance / Introductions

Who will be performing the introductions?

Suggested order of introductions:

1. Parents (usually introduced as Host and Hostess, Bob and Jane)

2. Siblings

3. Guest of Honor

Re songs requested, if not review DJ reference tool for a feel about requests on music options, and DJ style preferences.

Please list those to be introduced during the grand entrance in the order they will be introduced. You can choose different songs for each person or one for the entire group. Use additional sheets if necessary. If you want, interesting tidbits of information about relationships to the guest of honor can be announced—if so, please write details below each person's name.

For each name collect:

Name(s)

Phonetic Pronunciation(s)

How to Introduce

Music

## **Candle lighting**

A memory candle for deceased relative(s) may be lit by the guest of honor. Typically this is announced by the Guest of Honor, and is done either before the first candle is announced, or before the parents' candle is announced. Alternatively, one of the candles on the cake can be lit as a memory candle—this would be announced at the time of that candle. Will there be a memory candle?

Include the names of people who will be coming to the cake. Write the names as the Guest of Honor calls them and include phonetic pronunciation. The usual order for candle lighting is

1. Grandparents
2. Aunts
3. Uncles
4. Cousins
5. Older relatives
6. Younger relatives
7. Friends of parents
8. Friends of Guest of Honor
9. Parents
10. Siblings
11. Guest of Honor

The usual number of candles is 14 *(13 for age, one for good luck)*. Try to group relatives and friends together to keep the amount of candles to 14 as best as possible. You can have interesting tidbits of information announced as the individuals come up to light the candles. If you want to do this, please write details below each person's name.

You will also need to choose music to be played while people come up and light the candles. You can have one piece of music serve as background to all of the candles or you may want to match a specific song to each person or group of people lighting the candle (*preferably fun and upbeat*). The total ceremony takes about 15 minutes.

### Candle Lighting List

| Name(s) | Phonetic Pronunciation(s) | How to Introduce | Music |
|---|---|---|---|
| 1. | | | |
| 2. | | | |
| 3. | | | |
| 4. | | | |
| 5. | | | |
| 6. | | | |

## Events

Hora

Please indicate which family members you would like to be lifted in the chair during the Hora:

Kiddush

Who will be introduced to say the Kiddush blessing? Write the name as the Guest of Honor would, and include phonetic pronunciation.

Motzi

Who will be introduced to say the Motzi blessing? Write the name as the Guest of Honor would, and include phonetic pronunciation.

Toast

Who will be introduced to offer the toast to the Guest of Honor? Typically this is the father. Write the name as the Guest of Honor would, and include phonetic pronunciation.
Will there be other people offering toasts? If so, describe:

After the toast, will the Guest of Honor want to say something? This is a wonderful opportunity to welcome everyone and to do any special acknowledgements, such as guests who have traveled a long distance or friends or family who have contributed in the preparation of the ceremony or reception. This is a fun and memorable alternative to the typical, time-consuming receiving line.

Host/Hostess Dance

Song for host/hostess dance:
You can have us invite your guests to join in partway through the above song, or we can invite them up when the next song begins. When do you want us to invite other guests to join in?

Guest of Honor/Parent Dance

Song for guest of honor/parent dance (we recommend a slow song, some suggestions follow):

After which course (typically after main course):
You can have us invite your guests to join in partway through the above song, or we can invite them up when the next song begins. We can have all fathers/daughters and mothers/sons join you first and invite the rest of the guests to join in one verse later, or we can invite all of the guests to join in at the same time. When and how do you want us to invite other guests to join in?

For some people, a special dance with a Stepfather, Uncle, Brother, or close family friend is done in lieu of, or in addition to, a parents dance.

Grand Finale

Before the last dance, we can organize guests into a circle around the guest of honor, pass the mic around, and allow them to each offer best wishes. Do you want to do this?

Table Photos/Interviews

Please indicate the points (if any) during the reception when you and your photographer want everyone to remain seated for table photos:

Please indicate the points (if any) during the reception when you and your videographer want everyone to remain seated for table interviews:

If the photographer or videographer requests it, do you want us to clear the dance floor or delay the start of dancing for the completion of table photos and/or interviews?

Additional setups require:
Dedications, Birthdays, Anniversaries, Other Special Dances, etc.
List any special announcements you would like us to make. This is a great way to personalize your event and recognize someone special.

Additional Notes *(Use back or additional sheets if necessary)*
If there is anything else we need to know to ensure your reception flows smoothly, please list the details here. In particular:

- If you feel we need to be aware of Any sensitive information regarding your event, family, or guests
- If you are having a video presentation, a singer, musicians, fraternity/sorority serenade, centerpiece giveaway, or any other personalized additions that will make your party unique

# Large Conference Planning Budget Tool

While not easily depicted in print, we have built a spreadsheet tool to assist in tracking costs and budgets for a large conference, based on a number of factors including number of attendees at **products@newbizplaybook.com**.

| | # | $ | subtotals | Estimated Total | Actual Total | change +/- |
|---|---|---|---|---|---|---|
| **AV Equipment & Stage** | | | | | | |
| AV Breakouts: | 4 | $500 | $2,000 | | | $0.00 |
| AV General: | | | $0 | | | $0.00 |
| Set: | | | $0 | | | $0.00 |
| Labor | | | $0 | | | $0.00 |
| Stage | | | $0 | | | $0.00 |
| Video Production | | | $0 | | $2,000 | $0.00 |
| | | | | | | -$2,000.00 |
| **Venue Rental Fees** | | | | | | |
| Rental | | | $0 | | | $0.00 |
| Business Center | | | $0 | | | $0.00 |
| Set Up | | | $0 | | | $0.00 |
| Permits | | | $0 | | | $0.00 |
| Misc (biz center etc.) | | | $0 | | | $0.00 |
| Clean Up | | | $0 | | | $0.00 |

**Food & Beverage**

| | | |
|---|---:|---:|
| Cocktail Party: | | $0.00 |
| Monday | $0 | $0.00 |
| Tuesday | $0 | $0.00 |
| Wednesday | $0 | $0.00 |
| Thursday | $0 | $0.00 |
| Friday | $0 | $0.00 |
| | $0 | $0.00 |
| Meals: | | $0.00 |
| Monday | $0 | $0.00 |
| Tuesday | $0 | $0.00 |
| Wednesday | $0 | $0.00 |
| Thursday | $0 | $0.00 |
| Friday | $0 | $0.00 |
| Marketing Team Dinner | $0 | $0.00 |
| Meals | $0 | $0.00 |
| Décor (bill to dept xyz) | $0 | $0.00 |
| | | $0.00 |

| | | |
|---|---:|---:|
| **Offsite Night** | | |
| Party | $0 | $0.00 |
| Talent @ party | $0 | $0.00 |
| Gifts | $0 | $0.00 |
| Food & Drink | $0 | $0.00 |
| | | $0.00 |
| **Transportation** | | $0.00 |
| Agency Fee | $0 | $0.00 |
| Air | $0 | $0.00 |
| Shuttles | $0 | $0.00 |
| Auto | $0 | $0.00 |
| Buses/Limos | $0 | $0.00 |
| | | $0.00 |
| **Hotel Rooms** | | $0.00 |
| Lodging Single Rooms | $0 | $0.00 |
| Lodging Double Rooms | $0 | $0.00 |
| Lodging Suites | $0 | $0.00 |
| Pre-Conference Rooms | $0 | $0.00 |
| Staff Rooms | $0 | $0.00 |
| Site Inspection | $0 | $0.00 |

## Creative/Collateral

| | | |
|---|---|---|
| Design Fees | $0 | $0.00 |
| Placement Fees | $0 | $0.00 |
| Design | $0 | $0.00 |
| Main Gift - herbie | $0 | $0.00 |
| Notebooks | $0 | $0.00 |
| Brochures | $0 | $0.00 |
| Napkins | $0 | $0.00 |
| Centerpeices | $0 | $0.00 |
| Luggage Tags | $0 | $0.00 |
| Scrims | $0 | $0.00 |
| Disposable Cameras | $0 | $0.00 |
| Team Shirts | $0 | $0.00 |
| Invites | $0 | $0.00 |
| Photographer | $0 | $0.00 |
| Pillow Gifts | $0 | $0.00 |
| Chocolates | $0 | $0.00 |
| Decorations | 0 $0 | $0.00 |
| Stage Furniture | $0 | $0.00 |
| **Printing - Signage** | | $0.00 |
| Badges - Domestic | $0 | $0.00 |
| Badges - Intl. | $0 | $0.00 |

| | | |
|---|---|---|
| Signage Design | $0 | $0.00 |
| Signage Printing | $0 | $0.00 |
| Program | $0 | $0.00 |
| **Guest Speakers** | | $0.00 |
| Travel Expenses | $0 | $0.00 |
| Spa/golf | $0 | $0.00 |
| Speaker Gifts | $0 | $0.00 |
| Wine/Cheese to rooms | $0 | $0.00 |
| | $0 | $0.00 |
| | | $0.00 |
| **Event Labor** | | $0.00 |
| Registration Helpers | $0 | $0.00 |
| Uniforms | $0 | $0.00 |
| | $0 | $0.00 |
| | | $0.00 |
| | $0 | $0.00 |
| | | $0.00 |
| **Other Expense - Domestic** | | $0.00 |
| Receiving boxes/delivery | $0 | $0.00 |
| Tips to Hotel | $0 | $0.00 |
| | $0 | |
| | | $0.00 |

## Customer Tracking Tool

| Customer Name | Phone | Email | Address | Last Contacted | Last Ordered | Notes |
|---|---|---|---|---|---|---|
| | | | | | | |
| | | | | | | |
| | | | | | | |
| | | | | | | |
| | | | | | | |
| | | | | | | |
| | | | | | | |
| | | | | | | |
| | | | | | | |
| | | | | | | |
| | | | | | | |
| | | | | | | |
| | | | | | | |
| | | | | | | |
| | | | | | | |
| | | | | | | |
| | | | | | | |
| | | | | | | |
| | | | | | | |

## Event Signage Planning Tool

| Wording | number | size | placement location | placement 2 | notes |
|---|---|---|---|---|---|
| Agenda | 2 | 18x34 | outside classroom | next to registration | final version due X date for printing |
| Breakfast | 3 | 8x11 | | | make clear food set out is for this event |
| Lunch | 3 | 8x11 | | | place in plastic stands |
| Event Name +"Registration" | 3 | 16x20 | top of stairwell | bottom of stairwell | include arrow pointing right on one/left on other/none on the third |
| Phone Booth | 2 | 8x11 | outside floor one phone booth | | logo of old fashion phone and event logo |
| Registration A-G | 1 | 16x20 | above registration | | May need to HANG from ceiling |
| Registration H-P | 1 | 16x20 | above registration | | May need to HANG from ceiling |
| Registration Q-Z | 1 | 16x20 | | | |
| Restrooms | 2 | 11x14 | foyer | on ground floor | include arrow pointing right |
| Restrooms | 2 | 8x4 | place on bathroom door | | clever branding opportunity |
| Welcome (incorporate logo) | 2 | 16x20 | inside meeting room entry (on easels) | | |
| Cocktail Party | 2 | 18x34 | outside of tent on easels | in parking lot | include arrow for parking lot |
| Specialty Drink Descriptions | 2 | 8.5x11 | on bars in plastic holders | | |
| Attendee Gifts | 1 | 11x14 | outside meeting room at 5pm | | |
| Event Logo (purely branding) | 2 | 16x20 | in front of meeting hall doors | next to valet | need arrows pointing UP |
| Vertical Banners | 2 | 3x8 | placed outside meeting room after program | | vinyl and free standing, BLR Sign Systems |
| Podium Sign | 1 | 16x20 | mounted on podium | | |
| (speaker names) on large place cards | 12 | tent cards | on stage chairs | | print with Avery tent card paper on computer |

# Event Wrap Closeout Tool

As an event planner, it is very important to close out your events with detailed information you can use for future reference in the event you seek to use the facility for future events.

**Name of Event:**
**Date:**
**Chair/Event Producer:** Your name or the event chair
**Executive Host:** sr. exec that served as the internal champion
**Location:** name of venue, city, state

## BUDGET
**Event Budget:** Total allotted event budget
**Actual Budget:** $
**Any Major Overruns & Reason:** good to know
**Outstanding Payments/Issues:** list any disputes, outstanding major bills that may be en route, hopefully this is blank

## MARKET
**Target Audience:** such as: Chief Marketing Officers from consumer packaged goods companies in the mid-west region.
**Number of Invitations Sent:**
**Number of Attendees:**
**Actual Attendance demographics:** EX: 8 CMOs, 4 CEOs, 14 EVPs, 26 Directors. Or for a country club: 37 Current Members, 43 Recruits
**Highest Ranking Attendee:** Name, Title, Company

## COMMUNICATIONS
**Hard Copy Invitation:** Invitations sent 10 weeks in advance, tri-fold style, sent to 1200 invitees
**Email Invitation:** Soft copy invitation was sent from Liz Champaign 5 weeks before the event and again 3 weeks before the event to all who had not yet RSVP'd. Design created by Firefox Communications.

Confirmation Method: All attendees were sent a confirmation email immediately after they registered on the event website. All attendees also received a phone call confirmation one week before the event to answer questions and confirm participation.

Recommendations for future invitations to this event: What would you do differently?  Send fewer/more, different style, change the frequency of communication?

***If you can, you'll probably benefit from pasting a copy of the email invitation and a scan of the hard copy invitation to the end of this document.

**SURVEY SUMMARY:**

**Highest scored speaker:**

**Lowest scored speaker:**

   **Suspected reason:**

**Most attended breakout:**

**Least attended breakout:**

**Most popular activity:**

**HOTEL**

**Room Block Numbers:** 14 Suites, 109 Singles, 5 Doubles all days

**Actual Usage/day:** 13 Suites, 115 Singles, 4 Doubles on Tuesday

**No Shows:** 3 Tuesday, 6 Wednesday, 10 Thursday

**Rate:** $265 Suites, $119 Singles, $144 Doubles/night

## ACTIVITIES

**Golf:** 84 Signed up/96 Showed

**Tennis:** 48 Signed up/36 Showed

**Hiking:** 22 Signed up/19 Showed

**Recommendations:**

## EVENT STAFF

**Number for Event:** 14 onsite staff members, 6 were from J&J Temps

**Number recommended for next year:** Example: We would benefit from four more hosts at the golf tournament check in and a few more during the cocktail party registration desk.

**Quotes from Clients/Attendees:**
Share some great testimonials here received verbally or via email post event that your team, execs or future planners would enjoy hearing.

**Final recommendations for next event:**


**Photos:**
Add a few photos of the event that help jog your memory the next time around or help the next person. Centerpieces, signage, registration tables and stage sets are great to keep on file.

# Golf Events

Here are some ideas for hosting a great golf event!

Driving Contest

- Place judges on this fairway to cheer on your guests and keep score of the drives
- The pro can mark off milestones with flags prior to the Tournament beginning
- Each player gets three to five drives
- The top three drives count
- Works best on a long, wide, flat fairway

Longest Drive

- Guests who may not be accurate can show off their strength and ability to drive that ball down the fairway
- Works best on a par-5, long fairway

Shortest Drive
- Short is good in this case.
- Use the same par-5 hole as the longest drive contest, allowing more "winners"

Straightest Drive
- White line is placed down the middle of the fairway.
- The ball that lands on, or closest to, the white line is the winner.

Closest to the Pin
- Shot that comes to rest closest to the pin.
- Typically seen on a par-3 hole on the second half of the Tourney.

Longest Put
- Tiger Woods? Select a green with a challenging lie.
- Guests can place their ball as far out as they like, others then try to beat the leader.
- Works well as a pre-game contest, prior to play, great way for your guests to warm-up with friendly banter.
- If you have the budget, this is a great contest to pair with a marquee prize – the "Thousand Dollar Putt" or "Putt for a Buick".

## A

**Alcohol and Beverage Planning**, 37
Alcohol Consumption and Pricing Projection Tool, 37
Audiovisual Team, 21

## B

**Bar/Bat Mitzvah Reception Tool**, 72
**Breads**, 35

## C

**Candle lighting**, 77
**Cocktail Table**, 45
Customer Tracking Tool, 88

## D

Dance Floor Planning Tool, 50
**Desserts**, 35
DJ Reception Planning Tool, 68

## E

Entrance, 22
Event Signage Planning Tool, 89
**Event Wrap Closeout Tool**, 90

## F

Flat Fee Agreement, 12
Florist Interview Questions, 64
Flower Options For Weddings, 66
Food and Beverage Planning, 30
**Four months or more before**, 17

## G

Golf Events, 94
Guest List Management Tool, 51

## H

Hora, 79
Hourly Rate Agreement, 9
How To Charge For Your Services, 4

## I

**Immediately after the engagement**, 15
Important People Contact List, 52
Invoice Template, 60

## K

Kiddush, 79

## L

**Large Conference Planning Budget Tool**, 82
Linen Planning Tool, 43

## M

**Main Courses**, 32
Marketing for Event Planners, 24
Motzi, 79

## N

**Networking and Word of Mouth**, 26

## O

**On the wedding day**, 19
**One day before**, 19
**One month or more before**, 18
**One week before**, 19
Order of Events (please number 1-15), 49
**Other Event Planning Tools**, 71

## P

Packing Planning Tool, 53
Parking, 21
Percentage Contingent Agreement, 6
**Phone books, mailers and other print advertising**, 28
**Photographer Interview Questions**, 61
Planning Checklist, 15

## R

**Ratings and specialty sites**, 28
**Reception Planner Contact Tool**, 46
Registration/Place card area, 22
**Round Table**, 45

## S

Seating Planning Tool, 45
**Side Dishes**, 33
**Side Salads**, 34
**Six months or more before**, 16
Social Media, 27
**Soups and Stews**, 32
Stages, 22

## T

**Three months or more before**, 17
Toast, 79
**Two months or more before**, 17
**Two weeks before**, 18

## U

Understanding Your "Product", 3

## V

Vendor Contact Planning Sheet, 54

## W

**Website/SEO**, 25
Wedding Budget Tool, 39
Wedding Party Contact Tool, 47
**Wedding Shows**, 27
Week of Wedding Schedule Tool, 55

Made in the USA
Monee, IL
04 March 2020